FINISHING LINE PRESS

www.finishinglinepress.com

SUDDEN SHADOWS

poems by

James Lilliefors

Finishing Line Press
Georgetown, Kentucky

SUDDEN SHADOWS

ACKNOWLEDGMENTS

These poems first appeared in the following publications:

"After the Fireflies," "The First," "Wishes," *The Hooghly Review*
"The Purpose of Trees," "Motown Summer," *Door Is A Jar*
"Playing Tennis with the Past," *Rough Diamond*
"My Father's View," *Salvation South*
"Hope Came in April," *Pulsebeat Poetry Journal*
"Seduction," *The Passionfruit Review*
"Wild Blooms," *CandleLit Magazine*
"The Natural Order," *Crab Apple Literary*
"On Impact," *Front Porch Review*
"Nostalgia," *Third Wednesday*
"Chrysalis," *3 Elements Review*
"Hansel and Gretel (The Latter Years)," *Tangled Locks Journal*
"A Different Kind of Silence," *Ghudsavar Literary Magazine*
"Assimilation," *Ephemeras*
"Some Rooms are Prayers," *The Amethyst Review*
"Rings," *Moss Puppy Review*
"Shadow Boxers," *Roi Fainéant Press*

Publisher: Leah Huete de Maines
Editor: Christen Kincaid
Cover Art: Susan Greiner
Author Photo: Susan Greiner/Carolyn Greiner
Cover Design: Elizabeth Maines McCleavy

Order online: www.finishinglinepress.com
also available on amazon.com

Author inquiries and mail orders:
Finishing Line Press
PO Box 1626
Georgetown, Kentucky 40324
USA

Contents

To the memory of Janet Kay Lilliefors

After the Fireflies

Just after the last shadows fell, before the fireflies,
A strange light flared in the upper branches, a stillness settled below,
And I felt the weight of our lives quietly coming to rest.

We were made of what followed
What came before, of dust and stars, of stories
Told to take the place of what can't be known.

Walking under the trees into more permanent shadows,
You said there was something you would carry
With you, after the fireflies, so I would know.
Something visible, if just barely, as breath is in winter.

Last night, I think I may have seen it, high in the oaks:
A brief flame lighting the branches again.
And, later, may have heard: in the gust-driven rain
That knocked on the shutters and doors, as if wanting in;
A persistent sound, that couldn't be stopped,
That couldn't be answered.

The Purpose of Trees

During the storm,
you lost the shape of what you were,
forced to bend and bow,
this way and that,
in winds as harsh and unforgiving
as human rage.

Why did you just stand there,
in the face of such indignity?
I think I know the answer now.
You stood there because
that's what you do. Unlike us,
whose tendency is to flee.
You, who stood stoically for decades
alone, must have known that the storm
would quickly pass. That its aftermath
would be so bewitchingly calm it might
be perceived as a form of denial.

You stand now as living witnesses,
with wounds that defy epiphany,
the streets littered with your
broken branches, your smashed fruit.
You, who knew the storm
better than we did, stand to teach us:
how the will to survive
outlasts the will to destroy.

These are a few of the things
I might have told my childhood
friend, years ago, when he asked me,
"What is the purpose of trees?"

"To give us fruit. And paper.
To provide shade," I told him instead.
But after the storm, I know there are better answers.

In the divine mirror, we see briefly
who we are, then turn away and forget.
This, too, is the purpose of trees: to show us
what we don't remember we know.
You stand there because you are substance
and we are still mostly shadow.

The First

I knew you as I knew summer,
your eyes red-veined in the
chlorinated air, a wave of wet hair
pasted to your forehead
in the warm drying shade,
the two of us sitting cross-legged
on puddled concrete by the showers,
studying the lady bug that had landed
on the back of your hand,
its seven spots crossing
the water-wrinkled surface
of your finger and stepping
seamlessly onto mine,
as if they were parts
of the same hand.

You waited until it finally flew away
before telling me—watching with your
knowing, red-veined eyes—that the lady bug
had left behind a trail of good luck,
from your hand to mine, which could never
be erased, no matter how much we washed.

We were still children then, with no reason
to doubt what we heard. I did not yet understand
why people hurt other people. We did not know
what prejudice or privilege meant.
We did not worry about gray areas.
Neither of us thought your seizures
were anything serious.
Who could have imagined you'd be the first
person we knew who would go,
six weeks before your eighteenth birthday?

Playing Tennis with the Past

The problem with the past
is that it wants to seduce us,
twist, deceive, reduce us,
make us think we've outgrown it
as we're quietly arranging
the next tryst—care to hit a few?

The problem with the past
is that it's homeless,
desperate but rarely hopeless.
We are its hope, its host,
its sustenance, its mark.
The past knows our weaknesses
better than we know our strengths.
It remembers what we were,
and also what we thought we were
(or could be, or ought to be)
before it showed us we weren't;
not even close.

The problem with the past
is that it wants to be present,
but arrives out of order,
like a Burroughs cut-up.
Not even real. Not even past,
as Faulkner said—but always there,
the fractional moon that follows
when we travel, its uncertain light
spilling over nations that no longer
exist, their sovereign borders
worn away like the painted boundaries
of a forgotten tennis court.

My Father's View

My father's eyes were a strange blend of blue
—pale, cool, gently unflinching.
The blue of probability. His field.

The view from my father's study
was close, a second-story perspective:
maple leaves, phone wires, slanted roofs.
But my father saw far through that window
—far beyond what was visible,
past, even, what could be imagined,
to what was possible.

I never quite saw it myself.
But there were times, as a boy,
when I was startled by the reflection
in my father's eyes: bright morning,
snow tumbling down,
covering the world, waiting for footprints.

My eyes are still dazzled at times,
all these years later, by the ingenuity
of my father's view.
I look out and see snow
quietly collecting, unnoticed,
on the suburban streets where I live,
on the sidewalks, the bare maple branches,
and I pull on my boots
and go outside
to walk in it, while I still can.
To leave footprints.

Hope Came in April

When I was a boy, my father took us to see the Senators
play in twi-night double-headers at D.C. Stadium.
He wanted us to see the greats—Mantle, Maris, Yastrzemski—
and we did. But I was always more interested in the home team
—in men named Pascual, Howard, Valentine, Brinkman.

I brought a No. 2 pencil with me to keep score,
and a freshly oiled glove for foul balls, just in case.
I knew all the player stats, could recite them like a secret
language—home runs, batting averages, RBIs, ERAs.
Often my little brother fell asleep during the second games,
while my father sat quietly, occasionally scolding the players
to do better, the way he did my brother and me.

The home team always lost more than they won,
but we had something the other teams didn't have.
Our team's greatness, my father once said,
was its potential. And, with time, I came to see it, too
—to recognize flashes of greatness out there
under the warm lights at D.C. Stadium.
It was how, as a boy, I came to define greatness:
as something that appeared sparingly,
unexpectedly—but could change the world
in an instant, with one thunderous crack.

The year that riots burned our city down,
the home team won 65 games and lost 96.
Opening day was postponed that year
from April 8 to April 10 because a great man
was killed in Memphis, and angry people
were rioting in our city. My father tried to explain.

The funeral for that man was on Tuesday, April 9.
By then, D.C. Stadium had been turned
into a "staging area," my father said,
for the 82nd Airborne soldiers
who were in town to restore order.

The troops pulled out on Wednesday,
so the Minnesota Twins could take the field
for the 2 p.m. season opener.
We lost that game, two to nothing,
and the next two, as well.
But a week later, our team began a four-game
streak, and it felt as if something was beginning.
Hope was like that back then. It came every year
in April, when the tree branches thickened
with buds, when the breeze carried scents of hyacinth
and cut grass, and the whole city seemed to be waiting
to see what the home team would do.
If you listened closely on any of those afternoons,
you'd hear the sounds of fathers and sons, tossing
baseballs back and forth, generation to generation.
Our team never showed us how to win back then,
but they gave us that other thing, and for a while
it felt just as good: they taught us how to hope.

Fifty-six days after the season opener, another
great man was killed, this time in California.
Our team was in the midst of its longest streak
of the year at the time (five games). Seven months later,
they renamed D.C. Stadium for him.

I think of these things on a hot summer night
fifty-four years later, and a thousand miles away,
after reading the news online.
Remembering the luminous circular stadium
on the Anacostia River, with its lush green outfield
and dusty clay basepath that seemed as wondrously
alien and self-contained as a small planet.
Where my brother, my late father, and I sat in twilight,
eating salty popcorn from cardboard boxes,
drinking watery Cokes from tall, waxed-paper cups.
Where I learned to pay attention, to hope,
to recognize what greatness looked like.

The news story said nothing about those things,
of course. It didn't even mention the season
our city burned down, and opening day was postponed.
It said only that RFK Stadium was about to be demolished.
The news felt surprisingly personal, as if I was reading
the obituary of someone I had known,
and loved intimately, years ago,
whose death notice somehow left out
all the important details of her life.

Seduction

At dusk, the daylight
slips into something
more comfortable.
Shadows assume
the shape of desire.

You watch a plane
You're on the plane
The plane is you
There is no plane

Just like that.

Motown Summer

It might've been the hottest day
of summer, maybe the hottest
there ever was. A day when
the hornets and wasps
hid in shadows, fat and fuzzy,
sucking nectar into their crops.
And the Earth itself seemed
to crave something unattainable.

We set fire to that day
and watched it burn,
clearing the ground
of all that felt trivial or tired,
and drove on, through
the liminal landscape,
like fugitive arsonists,
leaving childhood
forever.

So why does that day still return,
long after those around it burned?

I remember the glass heat, vinyl sticking
to the backs of bare legs,
the faint gasoline smell on fingers,
the fruit-gum taste on your mouth,
the tinny sound of hope carrying
across the cornfields—a Motown song
that played on every radio in America
that summer, blooming extravagantly
for a few weeks, then gone.

A disposable day, a culture of
convenience: bottles, cans, dresses,
dreams; loyalties, friendships.
All could be replaced, in a way
that almost felt like freedom.

So why does that day still return,
long after those around it burned?
And what should we—knowing now
that our lives are largely fire—do
about the survivors?

The Wild Blooms
(a villanelle)

Not yet women, not yet men,
Ablaze with summer's fire.
The wild blooms were wilder then.

We fled childhood's outgrown pen,
Astride a crude desire.
Not yet women, not yet men.

To make small lives large again,
And history a liar.
The wild blooms were wilder then.

A shared heat, a secret yen.
To what did we aspire?
Not yet women, not yet men.

If we'd seen beyond our ken,
We might have risen higher.
The wild blooms were wilder then.

Than this sting of why, as when
Bare soles meet tarry pyre.
Not quite women, not yet men.
The wild blooms were wilder then.

The Natural Order

From a metal measuring cup, you
sprinkled seeds on every second paving stone
—black oil sunflower, shriveled corn kernels,
unshelled peanuts—along the path
between our house and the canal. Life followed
through the earth-smoke, like a private magic
show you conjured each morning
from the sky, the trees, the ground.

Always the squirrels arrived first,
followed by a strong-willed woodpecker,
while the jays watched from on high,
dive-bombing the whole-peanuts
and hiding them in tall tufts of grass.

The squirrels staked their claims without incident,
turning the peanuts in their agile hands
like Rubik's cubes, looking for a way in,
while the mourning doves took shifts,
displacing one another on the stones
like tag-team wrestlers, until the crows hopped in,
angry over something, and spoiled the party.
Often a wary cardinal waited demurely
in a tree, or a rabbit in the grass,
making sure it was safe first.
This was the daily feeding, the private nature
of the order you created.

What happened next, we didn't expect:
The squirrels, unable to tell time,
began arriving early, scrambling too eagerly
over the porch screen, sometimes bringing friends.
Then the woodpecker started its tapping
before dawn, like a prisoner rattling a cup
on the bars of its cage. Even the shy rabbits
showed prematurely, peering through
the porch screen like curious tourists.

And so we adjusted, beginning our days
with theirs, with coffee and a breaking of bread.
The world you created we lived in for a while,
like parents, providers of a new order.
And it would have gone on that way
—for years, we expected—if illness
had not callously swooped in.

It's eighteen months now since I stopped
the feeding. No one climbs on the porch screen
anymore, no one taps at the gutter.
They've all gone back to the wild,
to the natural order of things.

Sometimes I wonder if any of them
ever feels nostalgic for those days.
If, having known it once,
they ever privately yearn
for the return of magic, as I do.

On Impact

The late-October wind carries a
cedary scent of woodsmoke tonight.
I pause to draw it in.
Something is different.
A cold truth clings to the darkness,
leaves shiver brittlely
across the unlit landscape.

There are things to do,
and not as much time.
But time enough to wonder.
These are not my woods,
though I want to know them.
I want to know what lives here,
and what is coming.

I search for a column of smoke
among the trees but see only
my breath, turning to mist
on impact. I've lived several lives
already, the best of them with you,
and have this one left. I go on,
grateful:
They say we "gain" an hour
on Sunday. This year,
I'm going to be there when it happens.
This year, I want to see the old man
work his trick under cover of darkness,
and savor the gift of an hour gained
—even if it be a false hour,
even knowing the trickster will return
in spring, as we're sleeping, to take it back.
                    Here and gone, breath on glass.

Nostalgia

I feel nostalgic already
for yesterday, having sandwiches
with you by the water, in the shade,
not yet knowing how the rain
would invade so unexpectedly,
so spectacularly, glittering
like glass artillery shells
through the sunshine.
I feel nostalgic for surprise,
for the bracing ozone breath
of wet earth, petrichor, knowing
the difference now between then
and this. Knowing we'll never
know as little as we knew together
yesterday afternoon, captured
and then briefly captivated,
by an uninvited rain.

Chrysalis

Hope sleeps like
a dangerous thought,
waiting for the day.
But there are things
you must go through first:
The crucible of dreams.
The dreamless state.
The 3 a.m. x-rays.
The rattle in the hallway that
could be anything
(even death, you imagine,
rolling by on an old gurney).

Hope sleeps like
a dangerous thought,
but wakes
as something else,
the way volcanic
lava cools on impact
with air or water,
becoming black
obsidian.
How quickly we forget.
The obsidian snowflakes
glitter, frozen in stone.
Who says
we can't start again, today,
from right here?

Wishes

What happened to all those wishes
we sent into the skies of childhood?
Blowing-out-the-candles wishes.
Back-yard star-watching wishes.
Bedroom wishes, made behind locked doors.

Did they all just freeze and shatter
like helium balloons in the atmosphere?
Or did some find a higher frequency,
beyond the range of human detection?
Perhaps some traveled farther—deep in space,
like the pulse of neutron stars, silently sweeping
the universe in search of a place to land.

Perhaps. But I suspect most are much closer
than that—still here, orbiting invisibly
around our daily lives. And perhaps
they're why we're still here,
and why most of the things
that tried to kill us are there,
long-gone, lost in the darkness
that holds the stars.

Hansel and Gretel (The Latter Years)

There is a kind of weather that finds
the weakness in things.
That seeps through crevices,
scatters breadcrumbs,
blows past the borders of certainty.

A woman stands before a shallow creek,
her shadow darkening the water.
Late summer trickles by, a narrative stream.
Beyond the creek, the trees are dense and dark,
damp with dew. She smells bacon cooking,
and imagines a small house, its walls glittery
like sugar. But this forest is not a metaphor,
she reminds herself. The forest is a forest.
It's her way home.

In the house, a man stands before an oval mirror,
plucking hairs from his nostrils. He sees again
what the weather has done: widened and blunted
his once-beautiful face, buried it under layers of flesh,
writing sad wrinkles on the surface.
In his mind, though, he is still the little boy
who came here with his sister decades ago,
when the house was owned by an old lady
who caged the boy and tried to devour him.

Why didn't I just leave then? the man wonders.
It's a question he has asked many times over the years.
He looks out at the woods. The house is his now,
he feels safe here: *That's his answer.*

The woman sees a shape in the window
of the house she imagines. She thinks of her brother,
and, for a moment, of the woman she killed.
Their story came with such a facile ending:
All they had to do was return home,

to the woodcutter's cottage, and they'd be happy.
But in real life, you never forget abandonment,
you never forget how you got here.
In real life, there must be a larger story.

She has led several lives since then—wife, mother,
muse, tale-teller. But she still returns to this old forest,
to quiet her thoughts, to search for a better ending.

She worries sometimes what the obituaries will say;
how they will characterize her latter years.
Will they report that she and her brother had a falling out,
that they hadn't spoken in decades?

The man does not worry about such things.
He knows the obituaries will tell the tale
everyone knows and leave it at that.
He accepted their fates long ago:
She lives out there, with the weather
that finds the weakness in things; he lives here,
with what it has done.

A Different Kind of Silence

Her eyes stay with the crushed rabbit
in the road longer than I like.
As if she's never seen a dead anything before.
And then it occurs to me: maybe she hasn't.

Within seconds, my thoughts have moved on.
Nothing is said. I'm used to things
disappearing.

Weeks later, she is walking with me downtown
when a homeless man reaches for my arm.
We keep going. But her eyes study my face,
longer than I like. Nothing is said.

Everything at her age is a lesson.
I want her to be good: person, friend,
student, citizen. I told her once that silence
could be a good thing, a form of grace.
But this is a different kind
of silence, a silence of absence.

I, too, grew up without explanations,
and understand what saying nothing teaches.
The damage it can do.

But that's another thought
I allow to disappear,
knowing the world will
absorb this silence, and
none will be the wiser for it.

Assimilation

Then came the cheapening,
when even the air and the oceans
seemed to lose value.

Or—could it be they simply lost
interest, as many of us did?
Could it be that the tide, tired
of its same-old, same-old with the shore,
went out one night
and decided not to return?
And that the shore,
seeing it had gained ground,
sighed a breath of relief
and let the tide go.

It was remarkable, then,
how the wayward tide re-appeared,
sowing its oats in faraway ports:
There were sightings in the Seychelles.
On Bondi Beach. In Cape Town.
Seaside Heights, New Jersey.

Odes and anthems were penned,
singing the praises of what a tide
could do, and be, when free;
how far it could go.

Only the scientists harbored doubts:
If the tide had really broken free,
wouldn't it have been swallowed by the sea?
"Assimilated" was the word they preferred.

But the public, skeptical by then
of any five-syllable word,
just scoffed. And waited,
to welcome the prodigal tide

home. Gathering nightly by the shore,
giving absence a presence,
a value it never knew before.
While the real tide continued
to come and go, as it always had,
washing up privately on all the sad,
 secret interior sea-coasts.

Some Rooms are Prayers

The times they wanted me
to think their thoughts
and I went on thinking
mine.

The times they expected me
to hear, to see, to remember
a certain way, and I tried,
but couldn't.

Those times were rooms,
where people lived
and worked
and worried,
and loved and died.

I am surprised sometimes
to hear late-night voices
through open windows
and realize those rooms
are still out there.
Voices carry
answers to questions posed
long ago, to prayers spoken
—and not spoken—
in those rooms.
'Let us befriend fear that we
may know what it really is,'
they say. And I reply,
'Let us find the rooms that want us,
and learn to live in them.'

Some rooms are rivers,
winding a way. Some are
repositories, keepers of secrets.
Some rooms are circles,
always returning.

Some are sacred sanctuaries,
others just a stop in a station.
Some rooms are prayers,
some prayers are rooms.
No room is really ours.

Rings

I sat with you in the early afternoon,
as a beam of sunlight made patterns
across our living space.
Speaking as we did, now and then,
but in a way we never would
again. I touched flame to wick,
though you weren't there anymore,
and I wept in a way I couldn't
just an hour before.
In the peace of absence
came an absence of peace,
as unfamiliar as your lifeless
form now in the room.
All life is circular, you said.
Ecclesiastes. I thought about that,
before making the call,
then waited some more,
straightening your sheet,
your arms, your shawl.
The last thing I did
was take off your rings,
trying not to be rough—
the coming off not as easy
as the going on,
but easy enough.
Then I sat a while longer,
our lives in my hand, a perfect,
imperfect sphere, a closed circle,
as our cat slept on her cushion,
and the sunlight continued
to stream in.

Postlude

In these shadowed woods, a postlude plays.
Ripe with melody, remembered phrase.
A call to rest by familiar trees,
To breathe the air of remembered days.

Magic you made despite the disease,
With ten fingers and eighty-eight keys.
Playing preludes and postludes akin.
But just the postlude gets a reprise.

Preludes were meant to draw people in,
Say welcome, let the service begin.
Your postlude came with a deeper aim,
Not for the ear, for under the skin.

The tune started slow, a minor chord,
Stepped up to major, the chorus soared,
Then the coda, its notes played to pray,
Echoing countries, keys you explored.

I stop in these woods again today
To listen, stilled by the swish and sway
Of wind in leaves, of beauty at play.
Two years to the day you went away,
A simple thought now lives here, we find:

It's not what we make, take, win or say
That matters. It's what we leave behind.

Shadow Boxers

Here again, that strange time of day
when certain shadows of the past
meet less-than-certain shadows
of the future, unwitting partners
sparring dimly by interior light.

Our compulsions come out
to watch, with their vicarious desires,
before the shadows finally recede
again, into another day—or is it night?
The two always circling each other
like anxious prizefighters,
looking for a way in.

Reminding us, if only briefly,
what we started with.
What we have left: a lifetime.

James Lilliefors is a poet, journalist, and novelist. His poems and stories have appeared in *Door Is A Jar, Ploughshares, The Hooghly Review,* and elsewhere and he is a Best of the Net poetry nominee. He began writing poems in 2022 after suffering a heart attack and undergoing triple bypass surgery. *SUDDEN SHADOWS* is his first poetry collection.

Raised in the Washington, D.C. area, Lilliefors worked for many years as a journalist, beginning his career on the editorial staff of *Runner's World* magazine and later writing and editing for newspapers in Maryland and Florida. He was the founding editor of two newspapers in Ocean City, Maryland. He has written for *The Washington Post, the Miami Herald,* the *Baltimore Sun,* and elsewhere and for several years was the boxing correspondent for *The Cable Guide* magazine.

His novels include THE CHILDREN'S GAME (written as Max Karpov), THE PSALMIST, THE TEMPEST, THE LEVIATHAN EFFECT, VIRAL, and BANANAVILLE. He is also the author of several non-fiction books, including HIGHWAY 50, AMERICA'S BOARDWALKS, and BALL CAP NATION.

Lilliefors was the head writer at the Philharmonic Center for the Arts in Naples, Florida (now Artis-Naples), and has contributed to several books on art. He received his undergraduate degree from the University of Iowa and was a graduate writing fellow at the University of Virginia.